Breadsticks and Beyond: 50 Creative Recipes

By: Kelly Johnson

Table of Contents

- Classic Garlic Breadsticks
- Cheesy Parmesan Breadsticks
- Herb-Infused Olive Oil Breadsticks
- Cinnamon Sugar Breadsticks
- Pesto Swirl Breadsticks
- Cheddar and Jalapeño Breadsticks
- Garlic and Herb Stuffed Breadsticks
- Bacon-Wrapped Breadsticks
- Sun-Dried Tomato and Basil Breadsticks
- Italian Parmesan and Rosemary Breadsticks
- Buffalo Chicken Breadsticks
- Sweet Potato Breadsticks
- Mozzarella-Stuffed Breadsticks
- Focaccia Breadsticks with Sea Salt
- Spinach and Feta Breadsticks
- Bacon and Cheddar Breadsticks
- Cinnamon and Maple Breadsticks
- Truffle Oil Breadsticks
- Rosemary and Garlic Knots
- Almond and Honey Breadsticks
- Lemon and Dill Breadsticks
- Sourdough Breadsticks
- Roasted Garlic and Parmesan Breadsticks
- Zaatar-Spiced Breadsticks
- Prosciutto-Wrapped Breadsticks
- Sweet and Savory Fig Jam Breadsticks
- Eggplant Parmesan Breadsticks
- Sesame and Poppy Seed Breadsticks
- Caramelized Onion and Goat Cheese Breadsticks
- Smoked Gouda and Bacon Breadsticks
- Apple and Brie Breadsticks
- Veggie-Loaded Breadsticks
- Spicy Cheddar and Chive Breadsticks
- Mediterranean Olive Breadsticks
- Dill Pickle Breadsticks

- Black Olive and Parmesan Breadsticks
- Spicy Cajun Breadsticks
- Maple Bacon Breadsticks
- Sesame and Cheddar Breadsticks
- Sweet Pepper and Mozzarella Breadsticks
- Parmesan and Garlic-Cracked Black Pepper Breadsticks
- Roasted Beet and Goat Cheese Breadsticks
- Caramelized Onion and Balsamic Vinegar Breadsticks
- Pizza-Inspired Breadsticks
- Blue Cheese and Walnut Breadsticks
- Lemon and Thyme Breadsticks
- Sweet Churro Breadsticks
- Parmesan and Sun-Dried Tomato Breadsticks
- Herbed Goat Cheese-Stuffed Breadsticks
- Cranberry and Orange Breadsticks

Classic Garlic Breadsticks

Ingredients:

- 1 pizza dough (store-bought or homemade)
- 1/4 cup melted butter
- 3 cloves garlic, minced
- 1/4 tsp salt
- 1/4 tsp black pepper
- 1 tbsp dried parsley

Instructions:

1. Preheat the oven to 400°F (200°C).
2. Roll out the pizza dough on a lightly floured surface, shaping it into a rectangular or long shape.
3. Cut the dough into strips about 1 inch wide.
4. Arrange the breadsticks on a parchment-lined baking sheet.
5. Mix melted butter, garlic, salt, pepper, and parsley. Brush the garlic butter mixture over the breadsticks.
6. Bake for 10-12 minutes or until golden brown. Serve warm.

Cheesy Parmesan Breadsticks

Ingredients:

- 1 pizza dough
- 1/4 cup melted butter
- 1 cup grated Parmesan cheese
- 1/2 cup shredded mozzarella cheese
- 1/2 tsp garlic powder
- 1/4 tsp salt
- 1 tbsp dried Italian seasoning

Instructions:

1. Preheat the oven to 400°F (200°C).
2. Roll the pizza dough into a rectangle and cut into strips.
3. Brush the dough with melted butter. Sprinkle with Parmesan, mozzarella, garlic powder, salt, and Italian seasoning.
4. Twist the strips slightly and place them on a baking sheet.
5. Bake for 12-15 minutes, until golden and cheesy.

Herb-Infused Olive Oil Breadsticks

Ingredients:

- 1 pizza dough
- 1/4 cup olive oil
- 1 tbsp fresh rosemary, chopped
- 1 tbsp fresh thyme, chopped
- 1/4 tsp salt
- 1/4 tsp black pepper
- 1 tbsp grated Parmesan (optional)

Instructions:

1. Preheat the oven to 375°F (190°C).
2. Roll out the dough and cut into strips.
3. Mix olive oil, rosemary, thyme, salt, and pepper in a small bowl.
4. Brush the mixture over the breadsticks and sprinkle with Parmesan if desired.
5. Place the breadsticks on a baking sheet and bake for 10-12 minutes, until golden.

Cinnamon Sugar Breadsticks

Ingredients:

- 1 pizza dough
- 1/4 cup melted butter
- 1/2 cup sugar
- 1 tbsp cinnamon

Instructions:

1. Preheat the oven to 400°F (200°C).
2. Roll out the dough and cut into strips.
3. Brush the dough strips with melted butter.
4. Mix sugar and cinnamon together in a bowl. Sprinkle this mixture over the buttered dough.
5. Bake for 10-12 minutes until golden and crisp.

Pesto Swirl Breadsticks

Ingredients:

- 1 pizza dough
- 1/4 cup pesto sauce (store-bought or homemade)
- 1/4 cup grated Parmesan cheese

Instructions:

1. Preheat the oven to 375°F (190°C).
2. Roll out the pizza dough into a rectangle. Spread pesto sauce evenly over the surface.
3. Sprinkle with Parmesan cheese.
4. Roll the dough into a log and cut into strips. Twist the strips into spirals.
5. Place the twisted breadsticks on a baking sheet and bake for 12-15 minutes, until golden.

Cheddar and Jalapeño Breadsticks

Ingredients:

- 1 pizza dough
- 1/4 cup melted butter
- 1/2 cup shredded cheddar cheese
- 2 jalapeños, finely chopped
- 1/4 tsp garlic powder
- 1/4 tsp salt

Instructions:

1. Preheat the oven to 400°F (200°C).
2. Roll the dough into a rectangle and cut it into strips.
3. Brush the strips with melted butter and sprinkle with cheddar cheese, chopped jalapeños, garlic powder, and salt.
4. Bake for 10-12 minutes, until the cheese is melted and the breadsticks are golden.

Garlic and Herb Stuffed Breadsticks

Ingredients:

- 1 pizza dough
- 1/4 cup melted butter
- 3 cloves garlic, minced
- 1/4 tsp salt
- 1/4 tsp black pepper
- 1/4 cup chopped fresh parsley
- 1/2 cup shredded mozzarella cheese

Instructions:

1. Preheat the oven to 375°F (190°C).
2. Roll out the dough and cut into strips.
3. In a bowl, mix melted butter, garlic, salt, pepper, and parsley. Brush this mixture onto the dough strips.
4. Place shredded mozzarella in the center of each strip and fold the dough over to enclose the cheese.
5. Twist each strip and bake for 12-15 minutes, until golden and the cheese is melted.

Bacon-Wrapped Breadsticks

Ingredients:

- 1 pizza dough
- 12 slices of bacon
- 1/4 cup melted butter
- 1/2 tsp garlic powder

Instructions:

1. Preheat the oven to 400°F (200°C).
2. Roll the pizza dough into strips and brush them with melted butter and garlic powder.
3. Wrap each breadstick with a slice of bacon.
4. Place the bacon-wrapped breadsticks on a baking sheet.
5. Bake for 12-15 minutes, until the bacon is crisp and the breadsticks are golden.

Sun-Dried Tomato and Basil Breadsticks

Ingredients:

- 1 pizza dough
- 1/4 cup sun-dried tomatoes, chopped
- 1/4 cup fresh basil, chopped
- 1/4 cup olive oil
- 1/2 cup shredded mozzarella cheese

Instructions:

1. Preheat the oven to 375°F (190°C).
2. Roll out the pizza dough and sprinkle with chopped sun-dried tomatoes, basil, and mozzarella.
3. Cut the dough into strips and twist them.
4. Brush with olive oil and bake for 12-15 minutes, until golden and crispy.

Italian Parmesan and Rosemary Breadsticks

Ingredients:

- 1 pizza dough
- 1/4 cup olive oil
- 1/4 cup grated Parmesan cheese
- 2 tbsp fresh rosemary, chopped
- 1/4 tsp garlic powder
- 1/4 tsp salt
- 1/4 tsp black pepper

Instructions:

1. Preheat the oven to 375°F (190°C).
2. Roll the dough into a rectangle and cut into strips.
3. Mix olive oil, Parmesan, rosemary, garlic powder, salt, and pepper.
4. Brush the mixture over the dough strips.
5. Arrange on a baking sheet and bake for 10-12 minutes, until golden and crispy.

Buffalo Chicken Breadsticks

Ingredients:

- 1 pizza dough
- 1/2 cup cooked chicken, shredded
- 1/4 cup buffalo sauce
- 1/4 cup cream cheese, softened
- 1/2 cup shredded mozzarella cheese
- 1/4 tsp garlic powder
- 1/4 tsp onion powder

Instructions:

1. Preheat the oven to 400°F (200°C).
2. In a bowl, mix shredded chicken, buffalo sauce, cream cheese, mozzarella, garlic powder, and onion powder.
3. Roll the dough into a rectangle, spread the buffalo chicken mixture inside, and roll it up like a log.
4. Slice the roll into strips and place on a baking sheet.
5. Bake for 12-15 minutes, until golden and bubbly.

Sweet Potato Breadsticks

Ingredients:

- 1 pizza dough
- 1/2 cup mashed sweet potatoes (cooked and cooled)
- 1/4 tsp cinnamon
- 1/4 tsp nutmeg
- 1/4 cup melted butter
- 1/4 cup brown sugar
- 1 tbsp fresh thyme, chopped

Instructions:

1. Preheat the oven to 375°F (190°C).
2. Mix the mashed sweet potatoes with cinnamon, nutmeg, butter, brown sugar, and fresh thyme.
3. Roll out the dough and spread the sweet potato mixture over it.
4. Cut into strips and twist.
5. Bake for 12-15 minutes, until golden and fragrant.

Mozzarella-Stuffed Breadsticks

Ingredients:

- 1 pizza dough
- 1 cup mozzarella cheese, shredded
- 1/4 cup grated Parmesan cheese
- 1/4 cup marinara sauce (for dipping)
- 1 tbsp Italian seasoning

Instructions:

1. Preheat the oven to 400°F (200°C).
2. Roll out the dough into a rectangle and sprinkle mozzarella and Parmesan in the center.
3. Fold the dough over to enclose the cheese, then cut into strips.
4. Twist the strips and sprinkle with Italian seasoning.
5. Bake for 10-12 minutes, until golden and cheesy. Serve with marinara sauce.

Focaccia Breadsticks with Sea Salt

Ingredients:

- 1 pizza dough
- 2 tbsp olive oil
- 1 tsp sea salt
- 1 tsp fresh rosemary, chopped
- 1/4 tsp black pepper

Instructions:

1. Preheat the oven to 375°F (190°C).
2. Roll the dough into strips and brush with olive oil.
3. Sprinkle with sea salt, rosemary, and black pepper.
4. Bake for 10-12 minutes, until golden and crispy.

Spinach and Feta Breadsticks

Ingredients:

- 1 pizza dough
- 1 cup fresh spinach, chopped
- 1/2 cup crumbled feta cheese
- 1/4 cup ricotta cheese
- 1/4 tsp garlic powder
- 1/4 tsp black pepper

Instructions:

1. Preheat the oven to 375°F (190°C).
2. Mix chopped spinach, feta, ricotta, garlic powder, and black pepper.
3. Roll out the dough and spread the spinach mixture over it.
4. Cut into strips and twist.
5. Bake for 12-15 minutes, until golden and the cheese is melted.

Bacon and Cheddar Breadsticks

Ingredients:

- 1 pizza dough
- 1/2 cup cooked bacon, crumbled
- 1/2 cup shredded cheddar cheese
- 1/4 cup melted butter
- 1/4 tsp garlic powder

Instructions:

1. Preheat the oven to 400°F (200°C).
2. Roll the dough into strips and brush with melted butter and garlic powder.
3. Sprinkle with crumbled bacon and cheddar cheese.
4. Twist the strips and place them on a baking sheet.
5. Bake for 10-12 minutes, until the cheese is melted and golden.

Cinnamon and Maple Breadsticks

Ingredients:

- 1 pizza dough
- 1/4 cup melted butter
- 1/4 cup brown sugar
- 1 tsp cinnamon
- 2 tbsp maple syrup

Instructions:

1. Preheat the oven to 375°F (190°C).
2. Roll the dough into strips and brush with melted butter.
3. Mix brown sugar and cinnamon, and sprinkle over the dough.
4. Twist the strips and drizzle with maple syrup.
5. Bake for 12-15 minutes, until golden and aromatic.

Truffle Oil Breadsticks

Ingredients:

- 1 pizza dough
- 2 tbsp truffle oil
- 1/4 cup grated Parmesan cheese
- 1 tbsp fresh parsley, chopped
- 1/4 tsp garlic powder
- Sea salt, to taste

Instructions:

1. Preheat the oven to 375°F (190°C).
2. Roll out the pizza dough and cut into strips.
3. Brush the dough with truffle oil and sprinkle with garlic powder.
4. Twist the dough into breadsticks and sprinkle with Parmesan cheese and parsley.
5. Bake for 12-15 minutes, until golden and crispy.

Rosemary and Garlic Knots

Ingredients:

- 1 pizza dough
- 2 tbsp olive oil
- 2 cloves garlic, minced
- 1 tbsp fresh rosemary, chopped
- 1/4 tsp sea salt
- 1/4 tsp black pepper

Instructions:

1. Preheat the oven to 375°F (190°C).
2. Roll out the dough into strips and tie each strip into a knot.
3. Mix olive oil, garlic, rosemary, salt, and pepper.
4. Brush the mixture onto the dough knots.
5. Bake for 10-12 minutes, until golden and fragrant.

Almond and Honey Breadsticks

Ingredients:

- 1 pizza dough
- 1/4 cup slivered almonds
- 2 tbsp honey
- 1/4 tsp cinnamon
- 1/4 tsp sea salt
- 1 tbsp butter, melted

Instructions:

1. Preheat the oven to 375°F (190°C).
2. Roll out the dough into strips and brush with melted butter.
3. Sprinkle with slivered almonds, cinnamon, and sea salt.
4. Twist the dough into breadsticks and bake for 12-15 minutes.
5. Drizzle with honey once baked and serve warm.

Lemon and Dill Breadsticks

Ingredients:

- 1 pizza dough
- 1 tbsp lemon zest
- 2 tbsp fresh dill, chopped
- 1/4 tsp garlic powder
- 1/4 tsp sea salt
- 1/4 cup olive oil

Instructions:

1. Preheat the oven to 375°F (190°C).
2. Roll the dough into strips and brush with olive oil.
3. Sprinkle with lemon zest, dill, garlic powder, and sea salt.
4. Twist the dough into breadsticks and bake for 10-12 minutes, until golden.

Sourdough Breadsticks

Ingredients:

- 1 cup sourdough starter (fed)
- 2 cups all-purpose flour
- 1/2 tsp salt
- 1/4 cup warm water
- 1 tbsp olive oil
- 1/4 tsp garlic powder

Instructions:

1. Preheat the oven to 400°F (200°C).
2. Mix sourdough starter, flour, salt, water, and olive oil in a bowl. Knead until smooth.
3. Roll out the dough into strips and brush with olive oil.
4. Sprinkle with garlic powder and sea salt.
5. Twist into breadsticks and bake for 12-15 minutes, until crispy and golden.

Roasted Garlic and Parmesan Breadsticks

Ingredients:

- 1 pizza dough
- 1 head of garlic, roasted
- 1/4 cup grated Parmesan cheese
- 2 tbsp melted butter
- 1/4 tsp salt

Instructions:

1. Preheat the oven to 375°F (190°C).
2. Slice off the top of the garlic head and roast at 400°F for 25-30 minutes.
3. Squeeze the garlic cloves out and mash them.
4. Roll out the dough and spread the mashed garlic over it.
5. Sprinkle with Parmesan cheese, drizzle with melted butter, and twist into breadsticks.
6. Bake for 10-12 minutes, until golden and crispy.

Zaatar-Spiced Breadsticks

Ingredients:

- 1 pizza dough
- 2 tbsp zaatar spice mix
- 2 tbsp olive oil
- 1/4 cup sesame seeds
- 1/4 tsp sea salt

Instructions:

1. Preheat the oven to 375°F (190°C).
2. Roll out the dough into strips and brush with olive oil.
3. Sprinkle the zaatar spice mix, sesame seeds, and sea salt on the dough.
4. Twist the dough into breadsticks and bake for 12-15 minutes, until golden and fragrant.

Prosciutto-Wrapped Breadsticks

Ingredients:

- 1 pizza dough
- 8 slices prosciutto
- 1/4 cup grated Parmesan cheese
- 1 tbsp olive oil

Instructions:

1. Preheat the oven to 375°F (190°C).
2. Roll out the dough into strips and wrap each strip with a slice of prosciutto.
3. Brush with olive oil and sprinkle with Parmesan cheese.
4. Arrange the wrapped breadsticks on a baking sheet and bake for 12-15 minutes, until golden.

Sweet and Savory Fig Jam Breadsticks

Ingredients:

- 1 pizza dough
- 2 tbsp fig jam
- 1/4 cup crumbled goat cheese
- 1/4 tsp black pepper
- 1/4 tsp fresh thyme, chopped

Instructions:

1. Preheat the oven to 375°F (190°C).
2. Roll out the dough into strips and spread with fig jam.
3. Sprinkle with crumbled goat cheese, black pepper, and thyme.
4. Twist the dough into breadsticks and bake for 10-12 minutes, until golden and slightly crispy.

Eggplant Parmesan Breadsticks

Ingredients:

- 1 pizza dough
- 1 medium eggplant, sliced
- 1/2 cup grated Parmesan cheese
- 1/4 cup breadcrumbs
- 1 tbsp olive oil
- 1/4 tsp garlic powder
- Salt and pepper, to taste

Instructions:

1. Preheat the oven to 375°F (190°C).
2. Slice the eggplant into thin rounds and roast at 375°F for 15-20 minutes until tender.
3. Roll the dough into strips and brush with olive oil.
4. Coat each strip in breadcrumbs, then sprinkle with Parmesan cheese.
5. Top with roasted eggplant slices and twist into breadsticks.
6. Bake for 12-15 minutes, until golden and crispy.

Sesame and Poppy Seed Breadsticks

Ingredients:

- 1 pizza dough
- 1 tbsp sesame seeds
- 1 tbsp poppy seeds
- 1 tbsp olive oil
- 1/4 tsp sea salt

Instructions:

1. Preheat the oven to 375°F (190°C).
2. Roll out the dough and brush with olive oil.
3. Sprinkle with sesame seeds, poppy seeds, and sea salt.
4. Cut the dough into strips and twist into breadsticks.
5. Bake for 10-12 minutes, until crispy and golden.

Caramelized Onion and Goat Cheese Breadsticks

Ingredients:

- 1 pizza dough
- 1 medium onion, caramelized
- 1/4 cup crumbled goat cheese
- 2 tbsp olive oil
- 1/4 tsp black pepper

Instructions:

1. Preheat the oven to 375°F (190°C).
2. Caramelize the onion in a pan over medium heat with a little oil for 10-15 minutes until golden brown.
3. Roll the dough into strips and brush with olive oil.
4. Sprinkle with caramelized onions, goat cheese, and black pepper.
5. Twist the dough into breadsticks and bake for 12-15 minutes, until golden.

Smoked Gouda and Bacon Breadsticks

Ingredients:

- 1 pizza dough
- 1/2 cup smoked Gouda, shredded
- 4 strips bacon, cooked and crumbled
- 1 tbsp olive oil
- 1/4 tsp garlic powder

Instructions:

1. Preheat the oven to 375°F (190°C).
2. Roll out the dough and brush with olive oil.
3. Sprinkle with smoked Gouda, crumbled bacon, and garlic powder.
4. Twist the dough into breadsticks and bake for 12-15 minutes, until golden and crispy

Apple and Brie Breadsticks

Ingredients:

- 1 pizza dough
- 1 small apple, thinly sliced
- 1/4 cup brie cheese, cubed
- 1 tbsp honey
- 1 tbsp olive oil

Instructions:

1. Preheat the oven to 375°F (190°C).
2. Roll out the dough into strips and brush with olive oil.
3. Place thin apple slices and brie cheese cubes on the dough.
4. Drizzle with honey and twist the dough into breadsticks.
5. Bake for 12-15 minutes, until golden and the cheese is melted.

Veggie-Loaded Breadsticks

Ingredients:

- 1 pizza dough
- 1/4 cup bell pepper, finely diced
- 1/4 cup zucchini, grated
- 1/4 cup onion, finely diced
- 1/4 cup shredded mozzarella cheese
- 1 tbsp olive oil

Instructions:

1. Preheat the oven to 375°F (190°C).
2. Roll out the dough into strips and brush with olive oil.
3. Sprinkle the dough with diced bell pepper, zucchini, onion, and shredded mozzarella.
4. Twist the dough into breadsticks and bake for 12-15 minutes, until golden.

Spicy Cheddar and Chive Breadsticks

Ingredients:

- 1 pizza dough
- 1/2 cup sharp cheddar cheese, shredded
- 2 tbsp chives, chopped
- 1/4 tsp cayenne pepper
- 1 tbsp olive oil

Instructions:

1. Preheat the oven to 375°F (190°C).
2. Roll out the dough into strips and brush with olive oil.
3. Sprinkle with cheddar cheese, chives, and cayenne pepper.
4. Twist into breadsticks and bake for 12-15 minutes, until golden and bubbly.

Mediterranean Olive Breadsticks

Ingredients:

- 1 pizza dough
- 1/4 cup kalamata olives, chopped
- 1/4 cup green olives, chopped
- 1 tbsp olive oil
- 1 tbsp fresh oregano, chopped
- Sea salt, to taste

Instructions:

1. Preheat the oven to 375°F (190°C).
2. Roll out the dough and brush with olive oil.
3. Sprinkle with chopped olives, oregano, and sea salt.
4. Twist the dough into breadsticks and bake for 12-15 minutes, until golden.

Dill Pickle Breadsticks

Ingredients:

- 1 pizza dough
- 1/4 cup dill pickle chips, chopped
- 1 tbsp dill weed
- 1/4 cup shredded mozzarella cheese
- 1 tbsp olive oil

Instructions:

1. Preheat the oven to 375°F (190°C).
2. Roll out the dough into strips and brush with olive oil.
3. Sprinkle with chopped dill pickles, dill weed, and mozzarella cheese.
4. Twist into breadsticks and bake for 12-15 minutes, until golden and crispy.

Black Olive and Parmesan Breadsticks

Ingredients:

- 1 pizza dough
- 1/4 cup black olives, chopped
- 1/4 cup Parmesan cheese, grated
- 1 tbsp olive oil
- 1/4 tsp garlic powder
- Sea salt, to taste

Instructions:

1. Preheat the oven to 375°F (190°C).
2. Roll out the dough and brush with olive oil.
3. Sprinkle with chopped black olives, Parmesan cheese, garlic powder, and sea salt.
4. Twist the dough into breadsticks and bake for 12-15 minutes, until golden and crispy.

Spicy Cajun Breadsticks

Ingredients:

- 1 pizza dough
- 1 tbsp Cajun seasoning
- 1/4 tsp red pepper flakes
- 1/4 cup cheddar cheese, shredded
- 1 tbsp olive oil

Instructions:

1. Preheat the oven to 375°F (190°C).
2. Roll out the dough and brush with olive oil.
3. Sprinkle with Cajun seasoning, red pepper flakes, and shredded cheddar cheese.
4. Twist the dough into breadsticks and bake for 12-15 minutes, until golden and spicy.

Maple Bacon Breadsticks

Ingredients:

- 1 pizza dough
- 4 strips bacon, cooked and crumbled
- 2 tbsp maple syrup
- 1/4 tsp black pepper
- 1 tbsp olive oil

Instructions:

1. Preheat the oven to 375°F (190°C).
2. Roll out the dough and brush with olive oil.
3. Drizzle the dough with maple syrup and sprinkle with crumbled bacon and black pepper.
4. Twist the dough into breadsticks and bake for 12-15 minutes, until golden and slightly crispy.

Sesame and Cheddar Breadsticks

Ingredients:

- 1 pizza dough
- 1/4 cup sesame seeds
- 1/2 cup cheddar cheese, shredded
- 1 tbsp olive oil
- 1/4 tsp garlic powder

Instructions:

1. Preheat the oven to 375°F (190°C).
2. Roll out the dough and brush with olive oil.
3. Sprinkle with sesame seeds, shredded cheddar cheese, and garlic powder.
4. Twist the dough into breadsticks and bake for 12-15 minutes, until golden and cheesy.

Sweet Pepper and Mozzarella Breadsticks

Ingredients:

- 1 pizza dough
- 1/4 cup red bell pepper, finely diced
- 1/4 cup yellow bell pepper, finely diced
- 1/4 cup mozzarella cheese, shredded
- 1 tbsp olive oil
- 1/4 tsp black pepper

Instructions:

1. Preheat the oven to 375°F (190°C).
2. Roll out the dough and brush with olive oil.
3. Sprinkle with diced peppers, shredded mozzarella cheese, and black pepper.
4. Twist the dough into breadsticks and bake for 12-15 minutes, until golden and cheesy.

Parmesan and Garlic-Cracked Black Pepper Breadsticks

Ingredients:

- 1 pizza dough
- 1/4 cup Parmesan cheese, grated
- 1/4 tsp cracked black pepper
- 1 tbsp olive oil
- 1/4 tsp garlic powder

Instructions:

1. Preheat the oven to 375°F (190°C).
2. Roll out the dough and brush with olive oil.
3. Sprinkle with Parmesan cheese, cracked black pepper, and garlic powder.
4. Twist the dough into breadsticks and bake for 12-15 minutes, until golden and fragrant.

Roasted Beet and Goat Cheese Breadsticks

Ingredients:

- 1 pizza dough
- 1/2 cup roasted beets, grated
- 1/4 cup goat cheese, crumbled
- 1 tbsp olive oil
- 1/4 tsp thyme

Instructions:

1. Preheat the oven to 375°F (190°C).
2. Roll out the dough and brush with olive oil.
3. Sprinkle with grated roasted beets, crumbled goat cheese, and thyme.
4. Twist the dough into breadsticks and bake for 12-15 minutes, until golden.

Caramelized Onion and Balsamic Vinegar Breadsticks

Ingredients:

- 1 pizza dough
- 1 medium onion, caramelized
- 1 tbsp balsamic vinegar
- 1/4 cup Parmesan cheese, grated
- 1 tbsp olive oil

Instructions:

1. Preheat the oven to 375°F (190°C).
2. Caramelize the onion in a pan with olive oil and balsamic vinegar over medium heat for about 10-15 minutes.
3. Roll out the dough and brush with olive oil.
4. Top with caramelized onions and Parmesan cheese.
5. Twist the dough into breadsticks and bake for 12-15 minutes, until golden and caramelized.

Pizza-Inspired Breadsticks

Ingredients:

- 1 pizza dough
- 1/4 cup marinara sauce
- 1/4 cup mozzarella cheese, shredded
- 1/4 tsp oregano
- 1 tbsp olive oil

Instructions:

1. Preheat the oven to 375°F (190°C).
2. Roll out the dough and brush with olive oil.
3. Spread a thin layer of marinara sauce over the dough, then sprinkle with shredded mozzarella cheese and oregano.
4. Twist the dough into breadsticks and bake for 12-15 minutes, until golden and cheesy.

Blue Cheese and Walnut Breadsticks

Ingredients:

- 1 pizza dough
- 1/4 cup blue cheese, crumbled
- 1/4 cup walnuts, chopped
- 1 tbsp olive oil
- 1/4 tsp black pepper

Instructions:

1. Preheat the oven to 375°F (190°C).
2. Roll out the dough and brush with olive oil.
3. Sprinkle with crumbled blue cheese, chopped walnuts, and black pepper.
4. Twist the dough into breadsticks and bake for 12-15 minutes, until golden and slightly crispy.

Lemon and Thyme Breadsticks

Ingredients:

- 1 pizza dough
- Zest of 1 lemon
- 1 tbsp fresh thyme leaves
- 1 tbsp olive oil
- 1/4 tsp sea salt

Instructions:

1. Preheat the oven to 375°F (190°C).
2. Roll out the dough and brush with olive oil.
3. Sprinkle with lemon zest, fresh thyme leaves, and sea salt.
4. Twist the dough into breadsticks and bake for 12-15 minutes, until golden and fragrant.

Sweet Churro Breadsticks

Ingredients:

- 1 pizza dough
- 1/4 cup granulated sugar
- 1 tbsp ground cinnamon
- 1 tbsp butter, melted

Instructions:

1. Preheat the oven to 375°F (190°C).
2. Roll out the dough and brush with melted butter.
3. Mix the sugar and cinnamon together, then sprinkle over the dough.
4. Twist the dough into breadsticks and bake for 12-15 minutes, until golden.
5. For an extra sweet touch, drizzle with chocolate or caramel sauce.

Parmesan and Sun-Dried Tomato Breadsticks

Ingredients:

- 1 pizza dough
- 1/4 cup Parmesan cheese, grated
- 1/4 cup sun-dried tomatoes, chopped
- 1 tbsp olive oil
- 1/4 tsp garlic powder

Instructions:

1. Preheat the oven to 375°F (190°C).
2. Roll out the dough and brush with olive oil.
3. Sprinkle with grated Parmesan cheese, chopped sun-dried tomatoes, and garlic powder.
4. Twist the dough into breadsticks and bake for 12-15 minutes, until golden and cheesy.

Herbed Goat Cheese-Stuffed Breadsticks

Ingredients:

- 1 pizza dough
- 1/4 cup goat cheese, softened
- 1 tbsp fresh rosemary, chopped
- 1 tbsp fresh thyme, chopped
- 1 tbsp olive oil
- 1/4 tsp black pepper

Instructions:

1. Preheat the oven to 375°F (190°C).
2. Roll out the dough and spread a thin layer of goat cheese in the center.
3. Sprinkle the fresh rosemary, thyme, and black pepper over the goat cheese.
4. Roll up the dough and slice into individual breadsticks.
5. Brush with olive oil and bake for 12-15 minutes, until golden and slightly crispy.

Cranberry and Orange Breadsticks

Ingredients:

- 1 pizza dough
- 1/4 cup dried cranberries, chopped
- Zest of 1 orange
- 1 tbsp olive oil
- 1 tbsp honey

Instructions:

1. Preheat the oven to 375°F (190°C).
2. Roll out the dough and brush with olive oil.
3. Sprinkle the chopped dried cranberries and orange zest over the dough.
4. Drizzle with honey, then twist the dough into breadsticks.
5. Bake for 12-15 minutes, until golden and fragrant.